Introduction:

FIFTY YEARS AS A BRULE GUIDE

After a lifetime of trout fishing and guiding in the trout country of Northern Wisconsin, I thought it might be interesting to write about my experiences. I have been encouraged by my family and fishing friends to do just that.

A lot of what I have written is based on my years as a guide, especially those on the famous Brule for over a half a century.

At one time, I kept a fishing log of fishing days, size, and number of fish caught. I gave up this idea because it was too typical and statistical. It seemed more natural to write about those glorious days of fishing on my favorite stream with good fishing friends.

I did not want my career as an educator to influence my guiding, but to be accepted as a guide who knew and loved his work. This approach worked out fine, although sometimes I was called "the Teacher" by my fishing contacts.

It was my hope that I gave my fisherman a good day on the stream.

My favorite quote is:
"Time is the stream I fish on."

To Kay + Ron

1998

The River Brule: A Guide's Story

Chapter 1

GROWING UP IN TROUT COUNTRY

My story is primarily about my life as a trout fisherman and guide. I was steeped in trout lore at an early age. My father liked the sport and encouraged me to pursue it. Living in Northern Wisconsin after the big timber cut led to my exposure to trout fishing. For most of my life, my surroundings were close to some great trout rivers: the Iron, Flag, Fish, White, Cranberry, Muskeg, and many branch streams. And do let us forget the famous Brule River. The availability of this trout water was a most important influence. My father liked to live close to the woods and trout rivers.

Some of my contacts with trout fishing occurred at an early age. My father was great about taking me and my brothers along. Some of my childhood snapshots are of my father and his fishing friends fishing the river with wading boots, fly rods, and the split willow trout basket. The baskets were quite large and held large numbers of fish. I do not even recall these men talking about a limit of fish. I also learned to enjoy the tastse of trout!

Some of this early trout fishing took us to hard-to-reach branches of these streams. Some were only accessible by foot or by horseback on old logging roads. My theory was that the men thought the more remote areas were better for fishing, and they probably were correct.

I can recall one particular trip with Dad. He borrowed a

friend's horse and buggy for our destination on the Upper Flag River in Bayfield County. It so happened my father's work took him away from home, but on this occasion he was home for a few days. He said, "We are going trout fishing."

"But Dad," I answered. "The season doesn't open for a few days."

"We're going anyway as I have to get back on the job," was his reply.

We started early in the morning and made our way to his secret "trout place" via old logging roads. Upon reaching our destination, we made the horse comfortable, and proceeded to the stream. Dad had regular trout equipment; I had to cut a willow stick and attach my line to it. Of course, I was a "worm dunker." I thought about it as I grew older and wondered why he didn't make me a fly fisherman then.

When we were set to fish, I noticed something—a man's fresh tracks along the stream bank. I said, "Look, Dad, a man's tracks."

He said, "Some 'so and so' has been here first."

"Do you think it could be the game warden?" I asked.

"The warden never comes out this far," he answered.

We fished all day and never saw anyone. The catch was all beautifully colored "brookies." I know we caught a lot of them to take home. Our family and friends enjoyed eating these lovely fish.

Even at this early age, it was the trout and its environment that was so intriguing to me. I read everything I could find about trout fishing and equipment. I liked to look at catalogs of fishing equipment, especially pictures of the various trout flies. I learned the names of some of the famous trout flies. We subscribed to hunting and fishing magazines. I especially liked the trout stories.

Later on, Dad bought a Model-T Ford. This was great. We went to more distant fishing grounds—in spite of bad roads.

I tell these stories of my early life because this all had a great influence on my later life as a trout fisherman and guide. It possibly even influenced my career choice as an educator so I could somewhat have my summers free.

Fishing with Boyhood Friends

I spent some great boyhood days fishing in the nearby streams. I had some friends who liked fishing for trout, and we were able to borrow our dad's car for a day of fishing.

As boys, we were pretty much bait fishermen. These streams were pretty brushy, and only certain stretches were open enough to use flies. Later, when we were into fly fishing, we fished these open stretches. They were very productive, and we brought some nice catches home.

On nice summer days, we wore jeans and tennis shoes and did some wading. Early in the year, we used hip boots.

We used the telescope rods and simple reels. The trout basket kept our catch cool when we put in some moss or greens that grew along the stream. Occasionally, we would dip the basket into the cool stream.

My friends and I divided the stream area so we had some water to ourselves. We agreed on a meeting place for lunch and again at the end of the fishing day.

As I think back on these wonderful days, I realize how special these streams were. In season, we would have certain birds, flowers, wildlife, and berries to enjoy. It was a great place for a boy to grow up.

I chose to stay in the area and live. I did live in California for a year but it was not for me. I came back to the Northwoods.

Boy Guide

How did I become a fishing guide? No doubt, my interest in trout and fishing had much to do with it. Living in an area like Brule and Iron River played a very important role.

In my teen years, my folks built a fishing resort on a nice chain of lakes. A lot of fishermen came to stay in our cabins and fish the lakes. Dad was always busy building cabins. As the oldest boy, I was sent along to show our guests where to fish. I guess I was about 12 then and would spend days with these men. Dad taught me well and I knew my business. Of course, I was just "a kid," and they paid me accordingly. "Give the kid a couple of bucks." My father soon got provoked about the pay I was getting. We had a nice friend in the local game warden, Max Happle. He said, "I know how to take care of that situation." I was 14. He got me a special guide's license. I had a button to put on my hat. I was proud and could charge the going rate, which was about six dollars. Now I was a "guide." I particularly liked bass fishermen because they usually used artificial lures.

I still liked to get away to trout fish. One nice opportunity was to fish the White River. The Duluth Shore Railroad ran close to our resort. I could catch a morning train and fish until the three o'clock train, which would take me back home. I remember on one occasion that I was so engrossed in fishing that I heard the train whistle for Delta station but I didn't make it in time. I walked nine miles home. My father really laughed about this. I wrote it off as a great trout experience.

A nice family friend, John Casey, gave me my first bamboo fly rod. I never forgot his generous gift. I slowly started collecting more trout gear.

Another nice family friend, John Ziegler, took me under his wing and gave me a lot of valuable encouragement. John was a great fly-tier. He gave me my first fly book and a nice collection of flies. (I still have the old leather wet fly book.) John was a great Brule River fisherman. He took me along occasionally.

Another family friend was Dr. John Cumming—also a great Brule fisherman. He also took me under his wing and helped me get some equipment. The Doctor thought I should have other interests, and so he introduced me to golf. The "good" Doctor would take me away from the resort for fishing and golfing. My father would sometimes be concerned about me getting out of work but the Doctor was an effective persuader.

When I was old enough to drive a car, I would slip away to my favorite trout stream. Several of my school chums were from Brule. One of the fathers had a business and did some guiding. The other dad was a caretaker for a private lodge. This gave us access to the Brule and trout fishing. I learned some river lore about canoeing and what being a fishing guide was really like. I met a few of the experienced guides. Sliver Perkins gave me my first taste of the Brule by canoe. It was even greater than I expected.

President Calvin Coolidge made the Brule River known as he made his summer White House in Superior in 1928. This made an impression on me. Coolidge liked trout fishing.

His fishing headquarters was a beautiful place on the Upper Brule called Cedar Island. It had been built by Henry Clay Pierce, an oilman from St. Louis. Pierce was a great hunter and fisherman. He sent some timber cruisers, the Gheen brothers, to prospect for timber in Wisconsin and Michigan. He told them, "If you find a good fishing spot, let me know." The boys told him about Cedar Island on the Brule. Pierce bought about 5000 acres and started building a trout fishing place.

Pierce engaged a fish specialist from the East, E. M. Lambert. Lambert even started a small fish hatchery on the acreage. I had the good fortune to meet the man. He was a great fisherman and did Pierce proud in developing the rustic Cedar Island property and fisheries.

Learning the Brule

What good fortune: My first teaching job after college graduation was in Brule. I became friends with many Brule people. I began to meet some of the old-time guides such as: John La Rock; Ed and Ben Dennis; Max, Steve, and Rod

Weyandt; Basil Edgette; Dave Sample; and Trix Brevig. These men were experienced Brule guides. Most of the early guiding done on the Brule was for the private lodges and their guests.

Some fabulous stories were told about the fishing. One old guide told me about an ice house at Winneboujou. It was built especially for keeping trout. Large wooden trays were placed over long blocks of ice. I was particularly impressed by the size and number of native brook trout. The guide was not sure what happened to all of these ice house trout. I could imagine the fishermen got carried away with such good fishing.

I now had a chance to observe the beautiful hand-built cedar canoes. Handling these canoes was an art, and it was fun to watch these men paddle and pole the rapids. Their special canoes were good Brule canoes as they were not easily damaged on the rocks and rapids.

I got interested in spring and fall trout fishing. This meant big fish and generally bait fishing with heavy rods. It meant fishing the good holes in waders. It was another kind of fishing and, to me, not like fly fishing.

Some of the guides invited me on fishing trips. It gave me a real opportunity to learn guiding firsthand. These old guides had special techniques in fishing, canoe handling, and cooking. Observing their skills gave me a good chance to round out my education as a canoe guide.

I soon learned that many fishermen liked "seasoned guides." It was not an easy profession to break into. Many guides had spent years in perfecting their skill and some were not willing to take new men under their wing. I was fortunate to make friends with several good guides and, in so doing, advanced my skills.

After a short time, I had a list of some basic characteristics of a good guide. Above all, one had to be a good, congenial person. Also, one had to know the geographical area and the stream. One had to know some basic biology about fish and aquatic life, be a good canoe handler, and be versed in wildlife. A knowledge of the forest and habitat was important. One had to be a good basic outdoor cook. A guide had to be neat and clean, and be careful of controversial subjects. One had to carry a few basic necessities in your duffel bag. These qualities helped one build up one's reputation as a guide.

I remember one day when one of the younger guides was so elated that he said of one of the guests, "He asked for me!"

As I became more experienced, I fished with many fishermen. One group of doctors came for more than 30 years until they gradually all passed on. They were great friends, and I valued my time spent with these fine sportsmen. In many ways, they left their mark on the stream.

Bait Fishermen

Chapter 2

THE BRULE RIVER: A SHORT STREAM WITH A LONG HISTORY

The Brule River was named from the French word for burnt-over and is sometimes called "River of the Burnt Wood." There was a well-known explorer, Entinne Brule, but there was no evidence that he explored the Brule region. The name was probably prompted by the forest fires which burned out of control in the early days. It was sometimes called Bois Brule (River Brule in French). There are other Brule rivers in Minnesota and Michigan.

Dr. James A. Merrill, geologist, was an expert on local glacial geology. As his student in college, I spent some time in the field (especially in the Brule and Lake Superior areas). Thorpe Langley was a geologist and geographer, and a teacher of mine, as well.

According to geologists, the Brule served as an outlet to glacial Lake Superior. You can see these old river levels at Winneboujou on Highway B. When the glaciers receded, the river started its drainage system back toward Lake Superior. The main source of the Brule is a series of large springs close to the source of the St. Croix River. All along the upper river, one finds spring feeders and creeks. Farther down stream is the Big Blue Spring, Gaylord's Spring, Harts Lake, McDougal Springs, and finally the large Cedar Island spring ponds. These springs have a nice flow of cold spring water. It maintains a fairly constant summer water level. The quality of this Upper Brule makes it a fine brook trout fishery. The large spruce and cedar bogs help maintain this water by acting as a large sponge area, feeding and cooling the drainage.

Winter on the Brule

The upper river has a wild forested look. For the most part, the river has not been logged in recent times. Newcomers are surprised by the natural look the stream affords. No doubt, this also has a lot to do with the quality of the stream and its fishery. The land (especially Cedar Island) has old forest trees; some are virgin white and red pine.

The drainage is natural, and so no real flooding occurs. Some roads have added erosion problems that can be solved through proper drainage techniques. Some attempt was made during the Civilian Conservation Corps (CCC) days to improve the river with "wing dams." I am not too sure it helped; it did leave some unnatural looks.

Route of the Indian and the Voyageur

The Brule was a great link between Lake Superior and the St. Croix River as a fur trading route. Much has been written about the fur trading history. At that time, the Apostle Islands housed a great fur trading center.

The voyageurs carried very little for camping and left no debris. I suppose there were some more frequently-used camping spots if one knew where to look. As I fish and paddle this historical water route, it's fun to speculate about the Indians and voyageurs that used this river highway.

Over the years, I have looked in vain for signs of Indian habitation. Years ago, someone found a rock along the river at Cedar Island bearing the number 68. Could it be an old grave marker? I am told by some of the Chippewas in Brule that there are many Indian graves along the Brule on higher ground. The Indians summered here but spent winters farther south in Wisconsin.

John La Rock, a well-known guide, grew up on the Chippewa Indian Reservation at Odanah (near Ashland, Wisconsin). When he was seven years old, he made a summer trip from Odanah with his aunt to the Brule some 60 miles away. They walked on old trails. His aunt had a pack sack and carried a rifle. The trip took several days. Just as they reached the Brule, his aunt shot a deer for food. Somewhere near the Big Lake of the Brule, the aunt had an old cabin. Out in back, under a brush pile, was a birch bark canoe. They spent the summer fishing and hunting and picking blueberries. John remembered seeing many large fish, all brook trout, in the clear water of the lake and stream. They only fished for food.

Pioneer Fishing Families

Some of these families who owned private lodges on the Brule came to the river in the late 1800s. The Noyes family and the Holbrook family from Milwaukee came before the railroad to this area by going to Ashland and overland by horses—a pretty lengthy trip. This illustrates how ardent "trout people" can be. They established fishing lodges at first, and later summer homes when the area was more accessible. The accessibility came when the Southern Shore and Northern Pacific Railroads came.

At an early date, the Cedar Island Lodge was developed by Henry Clay Pierce (an oil man from St. Louis). Families from Duluth and St. Paul, Minnesota, were attracted to the Brule, such as the Marshall, Congdon, Spencer, Lindeke, Banning, Castle, McDougal, Ordway, Chisholm, Stott, Weyerhaeuser, Edeson, Gaylord, Connolly, Stewart, Enichen family, and those from the Winneboujou Club. They all enjoyed this great stream and its fisheries.

In retrospect, these landowners were very important to the Brule story. Their lodges were built in the rustic style to blend in with the Brule scene. Timber was not cut; the river was left natural. The owners were instrumental in keeping areas away from the river in a natural state, also. I think our forestry and fishery people could take a lesson from them. These trout lodges have been passed on to children and grandchildren who have the same respect for the river.

The lodge people observed the fishing laws, but they, as a group, set up standards on such things as limits and size. I admired their fishing rules. Their guests and families strictly adhered to these regulations.

Fly Fishing Preferred

Another thing I particularly liked was that they promoted fly fishing. I remember when spinning rods came in they were very upset about it.

The Stewart family came from Rockford, Illinois, in 1906. They fell in love with the Brule and purchased property at Stone's Bridge. They later acquired property known as Spring Lake—part of the Brule above Winneboujou. Steb and Gertrude Stewart were a great combination. Steb fished and Gert paddled. They liked the Brule and maintained their property as a natural part of the river. The Stewarts sponsored two top biology students in their Brule Lodge (Jack Hunt and Arnie Soli). They compiled some data on the Brule fisheries. The "fishing families" were serious about keeping the Brule as a natural trout stream. They used flies only. This family still maintains their Brule lodge.

Another Brule family was the Crosby family from Minneapolis. They had a nice fishing lodge a few miles south of the Brule near the old St. Croix trail. Their property has a beautiful stand of Red Pine, which they maintain in its natural state. They were all Brule fishermen and great boosters for the area. Beatrice loved the river trips with the fishing and lunch stops. The children still have this beautifully timbered property. Harriet Crosby, a daughter of Beatrice, recently purchased several large tracts of land not too far from the Brule watershed. Her plan was to leave it in its natural wild state.

The Presidents: Calvin Coolidge

Several United States presidents have visited the Brule. In my time, I am more familiar with Calvin Coolidge using Cedar Island as a summer White House. I talked to Emmett Lambert, Superintendent of Cedar Island, and Harold Swanson, and others. My best information came from John La Rock, the President's guide. Cal preferred John; he was a good guide and he did not swear. John found Coolidge to be a fine gentleman and an ardent fisherman. The one incident I liked best was related by John as follows:

Cedar Island was covered with security people organized by the very able Colonel Starling. When Coolidge fished, he was to be visible to security at all times.

On this occasion, the President said, "John, let's pull under this old cedar tree." John obeyed and soon whistles were blowing. Security had lost sight of the President. When it got looking real serious, they pulled out from the overhanging cedar and were again visible. John said he really got a dressing down from Colonel Starling.

John's statement was, "What would you do if you were given an order by the President?"

President Coolidge and Colonel Starling had planned a return trip to Cedar Island after the President retired.

I saw Coolidge several times. The Little Brule Presbyterian Church was a popular place to go to see him. Recently, I participated in a video of Coolidge's 1928 Brule stay, which was aired on a Duluth, Minnesota, television station. I didn't get a chance to see Herbert Hoover when he visited with Coolidge at Cedar Island.

An interesting side note: There was a small house in a back area of Cedar Island. I mentioned it would make a nice playhouse for my small girls. Swanson said, "Take it." My girls loved it. It was a unique little building. One could see it was for something special. Army security kept passenger pigeons in it when Coolidge visited the Brule.

General Eisenhower at Cedar Island

General Eisenhower

General Eisenhower was a guest of Jack Ordway (owner of Cedar Island at the time). He came to fish and relax. My friend, Harold Swanson, was his guide. I was busy with school teaching and missed being a part of the guiding party. At this time, people were encouraging "Ike" to run for the presidency.

Chapter 3

GREAT FISHING DAYS ON THE BRULE

<u>Serenity of the Trout Stream</u>

A part of canoe fishing for trout is the serenity of your surroundings. On the Upper Brule, you are away from man-made sounds, and only rarely an airplane flies overhead. It is easy to get lost in the wood sounds. The haunting song of the white-throated sparrow and the drumming of the pileated woodpecker on a dead tree or his raucous call is exciting to hear. Over the years, I have learned all the bird and animal calls: Hearing them is as much fun as seeing the birds.

As your canoe glides slowly through the cedar bog area, you smell the delicious woodsy scent of pine, cedar, and the many bog plants. There are some beautiful old-growth red pine and cedar in evidence; they tower above the deciduous trees. It is fun to think what it was like before the "big timber cut." The few that are left in the valley are homes for the eagle and osprey—yes, fish-eating birds, yet a part of this lovely scene. As we approach Cedar Island, we see several groves of virgin white and red pine. The one old record white pine at Cedar Island was finally destroyed by lightning. Also, in the area are some of the largest tamarack trees in the state.

A blue heron may fly downstream. Harold Swanson, caretaker and fish hatchery supervisor at Cedar Island, hated this "trout killer." I have a picture of a heron that was shot. Its stomach contained seven legal brook trout. This graceful bird is very much a part of the trout scene.

During special seasons, you watch for the lady slipper orchids and the lovely twin flowers—chokecherry and high bush cranberry blossoms. Usually, with one fisherman in the canoe, there is little conversation and the guide and fisherman are lost in their own sounds and sights of the stream.

We watch for fly hatches. Fish are rising. Do we have the right fly? We speculate—those rising trout look like good fish. We are in a position to fish to a rise. One is hooked. It's a dandy! "Play it carefully." Ah, a beauty for our live box. A nice moment of relaxing for the guide and the fisherman; one we will live over in our memories. While fishing with my long-time fishermen, I recall them saying something like, "Remember that nice one I caught under that old tamarack?"

Now with new limits in size and number, it is fun to speculate as we release some fish. Will we catch that one again? Most of my trout-fishing friends agree we need to have regulations. Each stream like the Brule has to be studied to make sure it is being handled correctly to protect the stream and still keep the sportsman happy. My thought is the habitat is most important of the two.

As our canoe slowly glides its way, we see new things around each bend. The silent canoe does not disturb deer that come down to drink or a bear that swims across the stream, or a wood duck that guides her little brood along the shoreline. Mink, muskrat, and an occasional otter watch us go by. High above the forest canopy is the beautiful osprey, and the eagle watches our approach from the large white pine near its nest. On occasion, a hummingbird has buzzed around my old red guiding hat—my personal trademark.

We come to a small cattail marsh and the male red-winged black-bird is on the watch. He gives our canoe a warning circle as we go by.

Next on the trip is a stop at Carl Miller's spring for a nice cold drink of water. I wonder if Carl is watching us and approves of our activities.

Today is the day that our rest stop is later than usual.

We will fish until dusk. My fisherman tells me this is the time for the "big ones." We proceed at a slow pace toward our landing. The sun has gone down. In the dusk of the evening, a new world surrounds us. The light has changed and the whole stream has a new look. As one friend would say, "It sure looks trouty." The wood sounds are different now. Later, we will hear the owl and the whipper will. It is nice to be alive and surrounded by all the wonders of nature.

We pull our canoe out just as it is getting dark. My fisherman and I are thinking (we don't say it), "What a great day!"

Working the Stream

On certain days, we worked hard for fish. It was fun to pit our skill against this wily adversary. We found a good fly and made a good cast and caught some fish. There was much satisfaction in picking up fish when conditions were not so favorable.

I have fished in Canadian and western streams in the 1930s and 1940s and was amazed at the number of trout one caught. I am sure these waters had large fish populations and possibly less fishing pressure.

One day while fishing the very upper part of the Brule, we met a very interesting fisherman. I will call him what everyone called him, "the Swamp Angel." He lived close by and fished from an old tin boat. He was parked where a little spring feeder came into the Brule. I said, "Mr. Landberg, how is fishing?" Without much of a comment, he pulled a fish stringer out of the water with some of the nicest brookies I have ever seen. Of course, he was bait fishing for food.

As a guide, you really have a time on certain days to produce fish. You try every trick in your book to produce something. We tried new flies, new spots in the river, and sometimes to no avail. Seasoned trout fisherman take this in stride, but the novice is hard to convince that we do have fish in the stream and generally make some good catches.

Some of my men have fished in so-called "virgin waters" and understand that time and place have a lot to do with successful trout fishing.

General Eisenhower Canoeing the Brule with guide Harold Swanson

Rain, Shine, or Snow

A good guide did not grumble on rainy days. You just hunkered down in the back of the canoe and make the best of it. Your fisherman has waited all year for this trip and, if he can "take it," so could I.

One opening day in early May, I was to guide Dr. Vernon Smith. It snowed that night, and in the morning we had several inches on the ground. My wife said, "You're not going out in this kind of weather, are you?" Of course, I couldn't disappoint the good doctor, so I sallied forth with my long johns and hunting pants.

We had a good day and caught some fish. We all agreed that our noon lunch was a great part of the day with a nice fire to warm us. As a guide, I did not like night fishing. It was generally cold and damp, and fishing could be very poor. At one time, the fishing rules closed fishing at 10:00 p.m. Most of the time, you were not bothered by other fishermen if it got to be that late. I guess it was the lure for one big fish that encouraged night fishing.

One great spectacle in the spring opening of the trout season was Sid Gordon wading the Brule with wool underwear, wool pants, and boots. I never could understand how

A Guide's Story

he could do it. He claimed he was comfortable. I think about the old lumberjacks on log drives dressed in the same manner. Sid Gordon was an outstanding trout man. He knew more about trout streams than anyone I had ever met. He has written some interesting articles as well.

Teaching Fly Fishing

Sometimes with "new" fishermen, a guide is put to the test. Where are the fish? The guide has to show these individuals where and how to fish. It was like coaching—"Put it by the log." It takes practice to do this, and you still have to know where the fish lie. One time, a first-timer was not doing well on a good trout day. In exasperation, he said, "Here, let's see you do it!" I had noticed a rising trout by a large rock. I put the fly on the spot and struck a nice trout. He was satisfied and listened to my coaching.

Not all of these men were good fishermen, but had a keen interest in the sport. I enjoyed helping them to become better trout fishermen. I found the women to be the best students. They listened to and followed instructions. Most men had preconceived ideas about fly fishing. They waved their rods too much and forgot the fly had to be in the water in order to catch a trout.

One man was such an active fisherman, his rod was going continuously. We named him, affectionately, "Old Buggy Whip."

Guides

On occasion, I fished with the other guides. It was fun to get away and do our own thing. We always had a good noon lunch with trout and the "fixins." George Sandman, Max and Steve Weyandt, Basil Edgette, Dave Sample, and Ed and Ben Dennis were great guides to be with. In later years, it was nice to be with Buck Follis, Jim Killoren, Roy Lyons, the Swenson boys, Larry Denston, the Spencer boys, and my nephew, Bob Berube.

I must say a few words about our Chippewa guide and friend, Carl Miller. Carl was a number one guide and an ardent fisherman. On his days off, Carl would go above Stone's Bridge to fish. He always came back with a nice catch to present to Ida Degerman.

He liked his little drink, but I never saw him out of line with his fishing customers. When he had a newcomer, he would stop at one spring for a drink of water. He made quite a deal out of this, coughing and hoping his fishing partner would produce a drink of brandy.

Carl served his country with distinction during World War I. He had a great following. Stories are still told about Carl. I took it upon myself to have a sign made and posted at Carl's spring stop. It simply states: "Carl Miller Spring."

Carl and his wife did not have children but raised several Indian orphans. When Carl passed on, the rest of the guides were proud to be his pallbearers.

I felt especially privileged to have a chance to visit with Antoine Dennis. He was probably the premiere old guide on the Brule. His colorful history made him a special person. He told his stories as they were. They are included in other parts of the book.

John La Rock was another great Brule guide. He had a wonderful personality and loved to talk. John could tell some interesting stories—with some exaggerations. Knowing John made me feel like a real Brule guide. John was generous with his guiding tips. I considered him to be my mentor.

A man called Sylvester was also a Brule guide of some note. He was called the singing guide. I never had the opportunity to work with him. He wrote a song called "Lilt of the Brule."

The House on the Little Brule

Some years ago, we built a retirement home—where else, but on the Little Brule and Sandy Run fork. I can boast that two trout streams cross my property. The Brule itself is just a few blocks away.

One of my fishing friends was an architect—Hilman Estenson. He helped us design a house that fit the Brule area, including a living room with large glass doors across one wall which looks out over the small trout valley. It's woodsy, and we have all the animals and birds that go with each change of seasons.

My oldest guide friend was Antoine Dennis, a Chippewa and a fine, interesting gentleman. He told me that the spot where I built my house was a famous camping place for Indians. I have looked for signs but have found none. My closest neighbor found an arrowhead. It is pleasant knowing they camped here and fished "my" stream.

I still qualify as a guide but, of course, not for commercial reasons. Some of my friends still contact me and exchange memories of "great trout days."

I did introduce some of my former students to trout fishing. They knew about my activities as a fishing guide and it was my hope to encourage them to be good sportsmen. One student/friend, David Goldberg, is now a businessman and owns and flies his own airplane. He fishes in Canadian waters, and I am happy to say he likes trout—especially "brookies."

I guess it's true you often lose the "big ones." My friend David Connolly and I were fishing a large flat area, and Dave was fishing wet. I moved in closer to where a spring came out in a narrow channel into the Brule. I knew it was a good spot. Dave got his fly in the right spot and there was a mighty swirl. He was into a big one. He is a pretty good fisherman, but he sensed he was into a good fish and he sort of froze. Of course, I was calling out instructions. "Dave, keep your rod up." Dave did not listen and, in a mighty splurge, his rod went down and the line becomes stuck. We lost a nice one. I say we lost it; after all, I am part of the team. He was a good sport, and we kept on fishing. We both will remember that one. How big? I think sometimes this is the kind of fish you remember more than ones that you put in your creel or live box.

Can you picture the following scene? It's a beautiful June day. My fishing friend, Ray Higgins, and his wife are my fishermen. The Higgens are Duluth people and have a love for the Brule. Ray is a good fly fisherman, and Mrs. Higgins enjoys the canoe and the pleasant surroundings.

It's a warm, high-humidity day. Looks good for brown trout. As we proceed downstream, we notice a few large green drakes emerging. What luck! I see a few small whirls along the shore—some nice fish are starting to feed. Ray fishes to a few spots. We strike some nice fish. We are close to one of the small lakes that are common to the Brule. We note a frenzy of feed where the lake meets faster and deeper water. The browns are moving up close to the silted area of the lake where the "drakes" are starting to hatch in large numbers—fish and feed everywhere, not jumping but taking the flies as they emerge to the surface and come out of their cases to dry their wings. I keep the canoe back, slightly out of the feeding area. Ray reaches out with his fly, and he gets a nice one. He leads the fish back to the canoe, and it doesn't disturb the other feeding fish. Some action! We take a fish on almost every cast, and they are all nice-sized fish. We lose count of numbers. Some are kept, and some are released. What a morning. We stop fishing as the hatch is over and the fish have moved back to their habitat. Fishing like this doesn't happen everyday. We count ourselves lucky. Ray summed up the day, "This is special in all of my trout fishing experiences."

Ordways

My early Brule guiding was for some of the people who had summer homes on the Brule. Of special note was the Ordway family. They acquired the famous Cedar Island property. It was all spring water and well stocked. It was a series of ponds that are connected through natural waterways.

They were all great fishing people and loved the river. Jack Ordway was a great fisherman and a most ardent trout man. I learned a lot from him, and I think I became a better guide because of his influence.

Jack Ordway didn't eat fish. This always amazed me. I enjoy eating trout and always saw to it that I had plenty. The younger generation is now enjoying the lodge. Jack's daughter, Sally, also built a Brule lodge. We caught a record brown trout at night, which is now mounted in her lodge.

Mrs. Jack Ordway was a nifty fly caster. She had good equipment and knew how to use it. Some years ago, she was in London and decided to go to Hardy's famous sport store for a new outfit. They were amazed as she asked to see a rod and then said, "I would like to try it out." She said eyebrows shot up. They went out in the alley where there was room to cast and set up a rod for her. Mrs. Ordway "gave it a go."

On one occasion, Mrs. Ordway was along to enjoy wild flowers and birds. Jack said, "Let's go see Old Nellie." (Now, Old Nellie was a special large brown trout approximately nine pounds who lived in the deep end of one of the ponds.) Mrs. Ordway said, "Jack, who is this Nellie?" We both laughed and told her about the huge fish. On one occasion, Jack hooked Nellie but did not land her. Harold Swanson, in charge of Cedar Island Fisheries, said Nellie finally died of old age.

He called me aside and said, "Lawrence, I have a special guest for you. He is the man who made 3M famous by his invention of Scotch tape. Without him our company would not be as successful as it is today. Show him a good time."

He was a very nice man. I asked him about Scotch tape. He said, "I guess anyone could have invented it." The secret was, of course, to make it sticky but still be able to peel it off the roll. We had a good day -- another great guiding experience for me.

Harold Swanson and Others

One special Brule family was the Harold Swansons. They

were in charge of the Cedar Island Lodge. Harold was a good trout man and operated the private hatchery. The sons, Emmett, Jim, and Jody, are good friends. They attended my school, and I was also their scout leader. We spent some happy days on the Brule. Esther, their mother, was a very pleasant lady and a good friend. Mildred Swanson was the daughter. She became a journalist and, when General Eisenhower came to Cedar Island, Mildred had an exclusive interview with him for a newspaper article.

As a scoutmaster, most of my activities were outdoor camping, fishing, and woods lore. It was a most enjoyable activity for me. I was paid a nice compliment by one of my scouts. He said, "Your teaching us fire building and cooking sure came in handy while we were in Germany during World War II."

I think every guide has some sort of trademark. Mine was a red wool hat. It took the weather pretty good, but it did fade and get a little shabby. One lodge owner used to chide me as I went by with, "Don't you think it's time you got a new hat?" I still have one and wouldn't go on the stream without it.

One fishing couple came from Milwaukee. Vic was an assistant superintendent in the school system. Betty had learned trout fishing from an uncle who was a Brule fisherman. They were great companions. Vic had one little departure from his usual flies-only approach. He had a special rod for worm-dunking when we got to Rainbow Bend, supposedly home for big trout. I went along with this. He never did hook into a big one.

Ida Degerman

One nice person who touched our lives was Ida Degerman. She operated the Valley Farm Resort. The resort had a nice farm-like setting, with a few rustic cabins and a neat log dining building.

Ida was a gracious lady and only wanted real fishermen

at the resort. Her meals were fabulous, and she packed a special lunch for our river outings. When she became ill in later life, the good Dr. Smith and fishing party brought her to St. Paul and did all they could for her. When Ida passed away, there was a Brule funeral. Dr. Vern gave the eulogy. All the fishing friends were there at the Highland Cemetery.

Bob North

I can recall one particular day with Bob North. We were in the Cedar Island area. It looked to me like a great trout day—overcast and warm. Bob was using our favorite dry fly. We noted a small hatch and immediately we observed rising trout. Bob pitched to where we noted a nice swirl of feeding fish. The trout literally sucked in Bob's fly. The water is a little faster here and it was a good fight. We had a nice brown trout. I held the canoe with my short snubbing poles, which prevented us from floating into the good area. Sometimes you can catch more than one fish in the same spot.

It was that kind of day that fish were feeding everywhere. We moved slowly and placed our fly near these feeders. We noticed a nice fish feeding on the downstream side of a large rock. We slipped by the rock and cast to its feeding. We out-foxed that one—a nice brown. It was becoming the kind of day a trout fisherman dreams of. The action continued until the hatch was over. The river became quiet. The fish were not feeding now. A newcomer might wonder if there were fish in the stream. Bob was expecting company at his cottage, so we kept some nice ones. Our companion guide, Buck Follis, paid us a nice compliment, "It's one of the nicest catches I have seen on the Brule."Some fishermen would tell me, "Call me when the hatch is on." Even so, the timing had to be right and then it is a thrill of a lifetime when you make the perfect connection.

Frank Young

Mr. Frank Young was another fine fishing friend from

Duluth. He called one day and said, "One of the top executives from our company is coming to town and wants a Brule trip. We have to have fish for our noon lunch." It was August "dog days" and fishing was bad, but anything for a good friend. The day before I had caught a few nice fish on the Little Brule near my house. They were in the refrigerator ready to eat. I took them in my lunch cooler that day, and at noon I proceeded to put on a nice fish fry (along with the few we caught). As we were eating, another guiding party came into our lunch spot. The head guide of that party called my companion guide, Jimmy, to one side and asked, "Where did you guys catch the trout? Jimmy said, "Oh, Larry knows where to get fish when the going is tough." We never divulged our secret. We had many good laughs over this incident.

I was guiding one day with several guides on the party. We had some younger family members along with the fishermen, and they took a shine to our Chippewa guide, Carl Miller. Carl knew they were watching him, and he was ready for a little show. "Would you like to see how Indians make fire?" he asked. Of course, they were eager. Carl went under an old cedar root and brought out a bottle whose contents he doused over the wood he had prepared. Carl lit a match and the fire lit instantly—kerosene, of course.

Pleasures of Guiding

Mel Ellis, a sportswriter for the <u>Milwaukee Journal</u>, spent some time on the Brule. He was a good sportsman and wrote about actual experiences. He wrote several outdoor books. In one of his articles, "Guides I Have Fished With," Mel said he thought I was a good fly caster. I was flattered but did not think too much about it at the time. I did not like a competitive attitude in fishing.

One of the best fish caught on a daytime trip was caught by a woman fishing with her husband. He was proud of her accomplishments. Not all men were picture-perfect casters but could get the job done and enjoy the sport.

As I think back, most of my days were good ones. As a guide, I made up my mind to overlook some unhappy incidents and be pleasant. It was easy to weed out the poor sports. Your best advertising was your reputation gained as you guided people. I received a letter one day addressed to "the teacher who guides on the Brule." My postman delivered it to me.

My story is not about "big ones" or fabulous catches but of pleasant days spent on a beautiful stream with nice people interested in trout fishing. I found a pleasant bond with fellow trout fishermen. As a guide, I was in my favorite surroundings. Every trout we caught was just as though I had the rod in hand. As the years went by, I met some wonderful people—many were world travelers who shared their travels with me.

We talked of other things. I had a background in natural science, geology, and the history of our area and could respond to questions concerning the Brule. I tried to answer the many questions concerning the Brule and not sound like I was an expert. Many things are discussed during a day of fishing. I recall one lady who was telling about the books she had read. She mentioned one in my favorite field. I was trapped. I said, "Did you read his latest?" She had not. I wondered what she thought, "Dumb old guide can read."

As I became more experienced, I could choose my clients and the days that I fished. This gave me more time with my family. Trout fishermen like to "go out early and fish late." This means a long working day. As guides, we hated to be stingy with our time but, in some cases, we had to have rules. We finally had to tell one group that these long days were out. As the years went by, guide fees were changed. Most of us were family men and the fee was important to our livelihood. We did our best to please and it usually paid off at the end of the day.

In one party with several guides, a wager was put up for

the best fish. My fishing partner, who was a nice man but not a big fisherman, got the prize. It was a beautiful large brook trout. He thanked me for my part and said, "This is one of my greatest fishing days." When he shook hands to go, a large bill was left in my hand.

A nice Brown Trout

Chapter 4

FISHING FRIENDS

Doctors All

One of my fishing friends was Dr. Vern Smith of St. Paul. Vern was both an outstanding fisherman and hunter. He was also an active promoter of good conservation practices. In addition, he was a great ski enthusiast and a wonderful photographer.

Dr. Vern and his party came several times a year. His friends were all good sportsmen, like himself, and they loved the stream and trout fishing as he did. The Doctor and most of these men have passed on. I have pleasant memories of days spent together.

I was invited by Dr. Smith on two Canadian fly-in trips— a dream come true with some of the best trout fishing I have ever experienced.

Most of my fishing friends were doctors. This was a good way for them to relax and forget the pressures of their practice. One doctor said, "If you ever get sick, call me." This life has kept me pretty healthy, and I have not had to call him.

One of my fishing doctors was Warren Cole. Dr. Cole was a world-famous surgeon. He loved fishing and, especially, fishing the Brule. He also liked to stand up in the canoe. One day he said, "You seem to be a very healthy man. Have you any health problems?" I thought a while and replied, "I have a terrible (as in big) appetite." The doctor said, "That is a sign of a healthy man."

Some Mayo Clinic doctors sent their head surgeon on a Brule trip. He was a pleasant man and brought his wife along. The doctor was not a very good fly fisherman but had the desire to learn. We were downstream a couple of miles on one particularly windy day when the wind took his line back around his body and the fly hooked into the palm of his hand. He became upset and said, "How far is it to medical attention?" I said, "Some 20 miles." I proceeded to pull the canoe along a rocky shoreline and then got out to check the situation. The fly was a #12 dry and not too deeply embedded. I grasped it between two fingers and easily backed the fly out of his hand. He thought this was great. I said, "Wait until you get my bill." We continued on for a nice day on the river.

Bob North

A regular fishing friend, whom I have mentioned before, was Robert North. He grew up in northern Wisconsin with a love for trout fishing. Bob lived in Maryland and was a lawyer and top executive with the dairy industry. He came every summer to fish the Brule. Our fishing association spanned almost 30 years. He and I have shared the pleasant task of building and repairing some Brule River lunch spots. Bob didn't like to call me a guide. He said we were fishing companions. "But Bob," I said. "How come white man sits in front of canoe and waves fly rod while guide sits in back and paddles canoe?"

Royce Dodge

Royce Dodge was a fisherman from Chicago. He loved the Brule and made several trips to fish each year. On occasion, I acted as his guide. He liked the Brule so well that he bought some land on the Little Brule, next to my property, and built a nice house for retirement. When the time came, he and his wife decided not to move up. A sad Royce came up to sell the house. Some time later, his best friend, Bob Zeller, came to Brule. I met him at the local restaurant.

"Bob, what brings you to Brule?" I asked. "I brought Royce back to Brule," he said.

Royce had passed away and his request was that his best friend bring his ashes back to his beloved trout stream.

Other Interesting People

Over the years, there were many guests of the lodge owners that came from other countries. They were not all interested in fishing but liked our scenic river and the idea of having a guide who was knowledgeable about the area. It was nice to get first-hand information about their lakes and streams.

During my years as a guide, I did take a lot of personal friends on canoe trips (some for fishing, others just to see the Brule). One older local resident said, "I have never been on the Brule with a guide." Shortly after this conversation, he passed away. I felt badly that I never got this friend on the Brule.

I have had a number of handicapped individuals on river trips. Two of these men were fishermen. I showed them a special day.

On a particularly nice fishing day, I was guiding a man from St. Paul. We had fished together before. Fishing was good, and the man showed great expertise. I said, "You sure are doing a great job and your fly casting is perfect. How did you learn that cast?" He replied, "You taught me that some years ago and I have been working on it." It was a nice compliment. As a guide, it was natural to offer fishing advice. I guess there were those who did listen to me.

I Tote the Canoe

One lodge owner that I fished with regularly decided to fish a more remote area of the stream. This entailed hauling a canoe up an old road and then hauling it through the woods.

There was a crude trail, but it was crossed with downed trees and logs. Most of it was through spruce bog and quite wet. We had complete gear for a day's outing. Our canoe was a 17-foot aluminum one. As I was getting the gear together, my fisherman took his fly rod and headed for the stream. I couldn't believe that he wasn't going to help with the canoe. I finally got down this torturous trail with the canoe and even kept my cool.

One question I have been asked over and over is, "Have you ever tipped over?" "Yes," I reply. "Once in shallow water. All we lost was our pride."

To quote an old guide's tale:
Some ladies told the guide, "I bet you know every rock in the river." Just then the guide hit one. "Yup," he said. "There is one now.

I met a very interesting man, Mr. Spielhaus, a famous scholar and scientist. He liked trout fishing and would ask in his British accent, "How is my casting?" As an educator, he had written about the American school system. He said, "What did you think of my article?" It was not flattering to our system but, trying to be a good sport, I said, "I am sure our system can stand your criticisms."

A great football player who was mentioned as an "All American" came to fish with me. Golam Jeske was a big guy and a canoe-full. We spent a pleasant morning and he said, "How about something to eat?" I mentioned the miles to our nearest restaurant. "Gosh," he said. "I thought there would be something along the stream."

During my guiding career, I have found some people who eat sandwiches in the canoe instead of a shore lunch. I guess they didn't want to waste any fishing time.

Did a fisherman ever hook me with his fly? Yes, but nothing serious. One man hooked my shirt so thoroughly that when he got home, he sent me a nice Pendleton shirt.

During a fishing day, conversation sometimes strayed to other fields. I stayed out of the political arena as much as possible but, on one occasion, a man that I knew quite well sort of pushed me in a corner. It was during the Nixon years. He asserted, "Nixon is not guilty of any wrong-doing." I took an opposite viewpoint. My other guide friend who was along said, "I guess you told him where the bear went through the buckwheat." The situation ended on a friendly note. The man I guided was called back to Washington, DC. I knew something serious was happening in the political world.

A Fishing Friend

I have to mention one nice friend, a Mr. Bell. He dressed for fishing in nice shoes, tweed pants, a little English hat, and vest. He looked like the pictures you see of a typical British fly fishing gentleman. He was a pleasant man to be with.

I was given the job of entertaining some people from the Minneapolis Opera. They were guests at a private lodge. Some lodge people thought everyone was a trout enthusiast. We managed to have a nice lunch and a good day without being too serious about fishing.

Some years ago, two men engaged me for a Brule trip and some fishing. I sensed they were professional men. They finally said, "We are with the IRS." I thought, "Oh, boy. They are even checking up on us poor, old guides." It seems they were on business in the area. They paid my guide's fee in cash and said, "That's the way we do it." They gave me a few tax tips.

Cedar Island Hatchery

George Beckwirth was an old-time "dyed-in-the-wool" Brule trout fisherman. He was a good fly fisheman but liked to boast about his prowess with the fly rod. One day after our lunch, he said, "I am going to guide you." I objected but to no avail. I figured out later that George had read about me in the column written by Mel Ellis, the sportswriter. The article stated that I was a pretty good fly fisherman. However, most of my time was spent with a canoe paddle, not a rod, and I knew I was a little rusty and this would put me on the spot. It turned out pretty well. In an hour, I caught more fish than he did the entire day. George said, "I figured you would catch that many."

An unusual event once occurred while fishing with George above Cedar Island. He cast to a spot where a large spring entered the river. He hooked a nice "brookie" and, while it was fighting, there was a mighty swirl and a large fish took the "brookie" in its mouth. It was a large brown. When George raised the fish near the surface, we could see the big trout with the small fish crossway in its mouth. I said, "George, lead the fish back toward me." I was ready with my net and as the fish neared me, I gave a lunge with the landing net and got this greedy fish. The "brookie" was about eight inches and the brown in the four- to five-pound class. The brown gave up his prize in the landing net. It was not hooked, but it did not want to give up its catch. I might mention as a footnote to this story that George had a strange request for his funeral arrangements. He wanted to be buried close to the Brule in the Highland Cemetery. George's burial urn was his old tackle box!

One of the lady lodge owners entertained her garden club, and the guides were scheduled to be around to take the ladies for short canoe rides. I took two of them around the lodge island. The rocks and logs were covered with plants, moss, and forget-me-nots. One lady noticed a particularly nice flower-covered rock and she said, "Did the gardener do it?"

Once I was sent out from one of the lodges to guide two nice young men for a day of fishing. I noted a skimpy lunch basket—three peanut butter and jelly sandwiches and a thermos of soup. What a meal for two men and a hungry guide.

Chapter 5

COOKING THE NOON LUNCH

A high spot in a day on the river is the noon lunch. There is nothing that whets the appetite like a morning of fishing. This is a good break from sitting in the canoe, not to mention the thought of some good food. Most guides are pretty good at this type of cooking. The smell of the wood fire, food cooking, and the coffee aroma is tantalizing!

Some typical menus are:

Bacon, scrambled eggs, toast, and coffee. If fishing is good, we sure save some nice "brookies" for an opening hors d'oeuvres. The bacon is cooked first, and the trout are cooked lightly in the bacon fat.

Beef hash browned with whole poached eggs on top is another favorite. Raw fried potatoes with onions is a good accompaniment with this menu. Thick sliced bread toasted also goes well. Bacon and a few trout are standard.

Steak on the open grill with the hardwood coals is special. Usually potatoes boiled with jacket is a good combination. Trout and crisp bacon served first as an appetizer produces a meal fit for a king.

Grilled pork chops and boiled potatoes is a good choice as well.

Spare ribs simmered in water for a short time and grilled over the hardwood coals is especially tasty.

Parboiled chicken is easy to cook over hot coals on a long handled toaster. The problem is keeping the chicken cold before cooking to preserve it.

Bratwurst is another local Wisconsin favorite, and

one can combine it with a variety of vegetables on the grill.

Good-old baked beans can be used with all the basic menus. A green that can accompany any of these meals is the fresh watercress that grows along the banks of the river. In season, corn on the cob is a great treat. Sometimes a lettuce or cabbage salad is an easy-to-make dish and the fixings can be brought in a cooler. Pickles and relish go with all the meals. Also, local fruit jams and jellies are a good addition for someone with a sweet tooth. Desserts are good but not as necessary with a fishing lunch. Cookies and cakes are easy to take along. Fresh fruit in season or canned peaches and pears make a nice easy dessert idea as well.

Bucky and Lawrence at Hidden Landing

Most fishermen are happy with the food, and we hear very little adverse comments. Some guests have ideas about better ways to do campfire cooking. It was not a serious problem. Some of the guests are good "camp cooks" and we usually include their special help.

On guiding trips from the lodges, we had more women to please. This sometimes required special handling and, being eager to please, we found some of the ladies were critical of our cooking. We tried to be good scouts and take it in stride. One lady objected to cooking the small trout with the heads on. She didn't like the looks of their popped eyes. It is well to state here that some of the women were great sports.

One man who was going to do a special thing (a cheese souffle) stood out in my mind. It did not turn out very well. He was embarrassed and took a lot of "ribbing." His statement was, "It always turns out perfect at home."

Glen Mellard was a great outdoor cook and a pleasant man to fish with. I called him my "toothbrush friend" as he manufactured toothbrushes. On one occasion, I saw him watching me as I cooked hash in a large frying pan with poached eggs on top. He said, "I wondered how you were going to get those eggs poached." I used aluminum foil to cover the pan. It did the job.

Do you like bacon crisp or lightly cooked? We served it crisp. Bacon is really a tasty lunch food. My one friend liked our bacon so well he asked what brand it was. I was proud to tell him we used a local brand, Elliots, of Duluth, Minnesota. He told me later he special ordered several 12-pound boxes from Elliots.

As I grew older, I had to watch my "outdoor diet." I cut down on the Swedish coffee and ate as little as possible of the fried food. This was not too difficult, and I tried not to be too conspicuous about it. Some of my fishing friends thought along similar lines but, of course, I was doing noon lunches more often—it wasn't just an occasional treat.

Cooking the Catch at Shelters

I guess in my book nothing is as good as a fresh-cooked trout. With built-in live boxes, you could control the number of fish kept. The fish were kept alive until cooking time. A lot of trout were carefully released before they hit the frying pan. What is a good day for a guide: To catch some fish and have a few for lunch. This made for satisfied customers. It would be out of line to say that all of the fisherman were like that. We had some that I called "meat hunters." As guides, we tried to weed out these fishermen. They were a small minority.

The noon lunch stop was a nice interlude for both guide and fisherman. We catered to the wants of individuals or groups. Good coffee was high on the list. I had learned how to make Swedish coffee with egg. It was allowed to stand awhile and brew. When ready, it looked like bourbon whiskey and was very tasty. I had one long-time fishing friend who really liked this coffee. On one occasion, his wife came with us. She said, "Why are you making so much coffee?" Ray, her husband, usually drank coffee at least during and after our lunch. I didn't tell her that her husband generally drank at least six cups.

Noon Lunch

Our trout were cooked "Brule fashion." The fish were cleaned, left whole, and rolled in a mixture of flour and cornmeal. A large pan with bacon was ready and, when done, the bacon, crisp, became an hors d'oeuvres. On occasion, we made a tasty sandwich with bacon, watercress, and onion on rye bread. The fish were cooked last—not overcooked— to a light brown and moist inside. They were served whole. A knife slit on the back opened up the fish, and one could remove the bones easily. This made an appetizing sight, especially with pink-meated trout.

The Brule has some special places to cook out. Landowners, guides, and fishermen have donated time, materials, and money to build some screened-in shelters and covered fireplaces. These were usually by a nice spring of water and made pleasant stopping places. We even built outhouses for our more particular guests. This was a pleasant time of day, and the morning fishing was discussed along with stories of other fishing episodes. The guides cooked and served the meal. We ate last. Cleanup was easy. We had grub boxes and cleaned the equipment to take home and wash later.

Many of our guests brought special things such as dessert. One day, a couple shared the first asparagus from her garden; another couple brought some brandied black cherries. My wife occasionally sent cookies or cake along. One good friend brought things to amaze me. One day, I said, "I suppose someday someone will bring ice cream along." It happened. Dave and Ed from Rockford had a special ice cream treat packed in dry ice for our noon lunch. On another occasion, Ed and Dave served "cherries jubilee."

I taste my own cooking

Did we ever forget to pack something? Of course. One outfitter, Ida Degerman, never forgot one item in all the years I knew her. She packed a great lunch box. Her bread, pickles, and jam were special. One of the guides decided to take home a glass jar of plums in his knapsack. On the trip home, the jar broke.

One fisherman who came to fish the Brule was the Robin

Hood flour man. He always brought a 50-pound sack of flour for Ida Degerman. Ida always provided home-baked bread for our lunches. One day while fishing with him, I remarked about the good bread. I honestly love home-baked bread. I quoted the old saying, "Bread is the staff of life." We were friends forever.

Two of my fishing friends took a trip to China, India, and Japan. The upshot was a statement on our first outing on the Brule. "You guides are cooking the fish too much," they said. After all the days I had spent with these men cooking fish for their lunch, I couldn't believe what they were saying. I tried to keep my cool and asked, "How do you want your fish cooked?" "Just put them in the hot grease and get them warm." I knew this new preference was related to eating sushi in Japan. The customer is always right. We tried to please. This method of cooking fish was not to my liking.

An amusing incident happened at our noon lunches. A new guide was asked to go up in the spring and bring back some watercress. He returned with a collection of cress, forget-me-not flowers, and several other water plants. One guest said, "That's some salad! What is it?" We said, "It's a Brule salad."

Another story at our noon lunch concerned our two oldest guides, Basil and Carl. One of the guests had to have a soft-boiled egg. Carl had his watch out to time it. Basil said, "You can't use the same time at this lunch ground as you do up river at Buckhorn." Carl asked why. Basil replied, "Because of the difference in elevation."

Ejected from the Lunch Site

The Upper Brule has a number of picnic stops. These belonged to the many private lodges. Years ago when it was difficult to haul canoes, guides poled canoes up the river. These spots bore the name of the lodge that had constructed the shelters and cooking places. Strange as it may seem, most of the lodges had constructed these shelters on someone else's property. It was assumed that each lodge would use its own picnic spot.

My fellow guide, John La Rock, and I had some guests from a private lodge. The lady hostess decided to go to another spot that was used by another lodge. Everything was going well until we noticed two canoes heading for the spot we selected. We had a fire going and bacon and coffee cooking. A man in the lead canoe said, "You're using my picnic spot, and I want you to move." John and I looked to our hostess, expecting some explosive statements—she was well-known for a quick temper. She very calmly told John and I to pack up our things and move to another place, hot frying pan and all. John and I were of the opinion that the party could have waited until we had our lunch. We still had a nice outing, however.

One of my lodge owner friends had a special river party—no fishing; just canoeing and lunch. The lunch was very special and even the butler came along. He and I were getting the food ready when I noticed the butler was a "little green around the gills." He evidently had gotten into the dinner wine. I told him to go back in the cedar grove and take it easy.

The host soon came to the cooking area and asked, "Where is Rudolph?" I told him what had happened. He was a good sport and very understanding about the situation.

One lodge owner liked to take his whole family on a Brule outing. This involved several canoes and guides. It was always well planned, and a good outing for the guides. On one occasion, we arrived at our mid-destination—Buckhorn picnic grounds. Everyone was helping. The meal was usually big and something very special. I suddenly noticed the main meat course was missing. One of the son-in-laws had forgotten it in the trunk of his car at Stone's Landing (some four miles up river). Two of the younger fellows paddled back and brought the main course. Everyone took it in stride, and we proceeded to have a great day.

Bring on the Bear

One man had fished the Brule many times in his younger years. He lived in a large Wisconsin city and made yearly visits to the Brule. On one occasion, he brought his young wife who was very pregnant. At the start of our fishing, she asked if we ever saw bear. She was a good sport and enjoyed the river. We stopped at our Hidden Campground for lunch. The cooking area is separate from the little screenhouse where we ate. As we were having our meal, I glanced out at our fireplace. Mr. Bear was there. He picked up our frying pan with his front paws. Standing on his hind legs, he walked off into the woods and proceeded to clean out the pan. The man was able to get a nice picture of Mr. Bear.

A family group at Hidden

Hidden Campground Destroyed

In the 1980s, a windstorm swept down the valley and destroyed our hidden lunch place. We decided to rebuild it. Bob North and I headed up an effort to raise money. We contacted all of our fishing friends. The results were great. We had enough to rebuild and some money left over for repairs on some other shelters. A contractor, Gary Peterson, came to our rescue and put up a neat, rustic shelter and cookhouse. This is open to the public. You take your turn. Some signs were placed to encourage everyone to keep it clean. Edson Gaylord had a special stove made for cooking at the site. The Ordways must be credited for letting us use their property at Hidden Campground. Jean Adams, a great fisherwoman from Rockford, Illinois, left us a nice fund for repairs in her will. This speaks well for our trout fishing friends and their love for the Brule. Jean's daughter, Nancy, also fishes the Brule.

Keeping the River and Campsites Clean

The lunch places are open to the public on a first-come basis. If you had room, you could invite the party to join you; otherwise, they must wait until you finished your lunch. An important step is "Take your garbage with you."

Keeping the river and campsites clean sometimes poses a problem. Some men had careless habits with cigarettes and other disposable items. They had to be told (even if it was a touchy subject). One noon hour as I cleaned trout, I checked some fish stomachs—sure enough, there was a plastic cigarette filter in one fish. I showed it to the fisherman and explained this could be a serious problem for fish.

As canoe traffic increased, we found disposable cans to be a serious problem. It spoiled the whole Brule scene to see a can along the shoreline. With the help of our DNR, we posted signs at launching spots. It helped. I carried a long-handled net and sometimes retrieved a few of these items. Educating people about environmental issues is quite a task. Some people would leave their disposable items in neat garbage bags thinking some kindly ranger would pick it up. Our motto was "If you brought it, you can take it home."

We now have signs saying "Catch and release your fish." Also, certain size fish, such as spawners, are protected. It is another matter to educate the public to do this. Some released fish are bound to die if not handled carefully.

Chapter 6

BRULE TROUT: BROOK, BROWN, RAINBOW, AND SALMON

The native Brule River fish is the brook trout. As the glacier retreated, it left many cold, clear streams suitable for the development of the brook trout. The only fish that is like the brookie is the Arctic char. As the past glacial climate changed, the brook trout was found in only clear, cold water streams and lakes. This trout is very catchable, and thus its population is easily reduced. It will take any kind of bait or most flies and artificial lures. I think it is one of the most beautiful of all fish. I have an old "stone cut" picture that is my favorite. It is of a great fighter on the line. I have fished several Canadian waters just for brook trout. It is my favorite fish to eat—especially cooked "Brule style" (see section on noon lunches).

One of the problems today is lack of suitable habitat for the brook trout. Water temperature is crucial. This fish also needs a special gravel bottom for spawn. Many of our streams have become silted, covering the good spawning areas. Some stream improvements have helped, and biologists have even created spawning beds by bringing in gravel. I have been told by hatchery experts that the brookie is difficult to raise. It is susceptible to several diseases.

When brown trout and rainbow were introduced, it changed the trout picture. Competition for spawning areas, habitat, and food affected the brook trout in particular. Now we have introduced the salmon, another competitor.

When the brookie was the only trout inhabitating the Brule, there were stories of large catches—sometimes 50 per day when there were no restrictions. The average size was much larger than today. The Brule, like other streams, could not supply this kind of fish forever. Just a few years ago, in my time, one could catch 25 for a daily limit. Present day regulations of size and number have helped some to stabilize fish populations.

One can still find some nice brookies in Lake Superior, especially some shorelines near Washburn and Bayfield, Wisconsin and they are called "coasters." They show very little color until they go up streams like the Brule and spawn. This spawning of the lake-run brookies seems very limited today.

The brown, rainbow, and salmon are all sport fish but are migratory and spend much of the time in Lake Superior. Brown trout stay in the river longer than the other migrants and become a good sport fish for fly fishermen.

The large rainbows, browns, and salmon are fished in the lower river during the fall and spring season and are caught mostly by bait fishing.

Flies: Wet or Dry?

I have decided not to be too technical about the trout equipment, but a few words about trout flies might be in order.

All flies are made to imitate some natural insect that trout feed upon. Most of the flies on the river are hatches in the stream bottom. Many are in little cases that come to the surface and release a flying insect. The fish feed on these under the water and on top when it opens the wings to fly. The adults live just long enough to mate and lay eggs in the stream where they go through the life cycle.

Fishermen generally fish wet (a "sinking fly") or dry (a "floating fly"). The fly tier's goal is to create a fly that looks like a stage of a natural insect either wet or dry. These insects come from the stream bottom as a larva. They rise to the top and spread their wings to fly along the stream to propagate. The fish takes them underwater and also when they fly along the surface. A fisherman can choose underwater (wet flies) or a winged (dry fly) on the surface, thus a choice of wet pattern or dry pattern fishing. In my own fishing, I never got into wet versus dry fishing: A nice-fighting trout on your rod is fun in either case.

There is some controversy over fishing either wet or dry. It is noted that the dry fly fisherman thinks he is the purist. It is my observation that each type requires special equipment and special skills. I have found that a fly tied by an expert is the answer to good fly fishing.

Flies that tend to work well on the Brule are dries (Irrestibles, Rat Faced McDougal, Coachmen, Wolf, and Hendrickson) and wets (Coachmen, Pass Lake Muddler, Hares Ear, and various other streamers). Of course, some are better for browns, brooks, or rainbows. Rod, reels, and lines are up to the individual fishermen.

How you fish the fly is most important. This is a technique learned well by only a few. Also, part of the art of fly fishing is being able to "read the water." By experience, you learn where to place the fly. A good fishing guide can be of help in this skill. Next comes the most important technique: "setting" or "striking" the fish. Experience improves this. However, I have fished with many who have not mastered this important part of fly fishing. It is important to relax, have fun, and enjoy the sport. Expertise will come after this. An Iowa-born cousin who loved fishing and was a sharp lawyer said on one occasion when he wasn't doing too well in striking or catching, "I didn't think fish were that smart."

Night Fishing for Big Browns

Night fishing is a special form of fishing on the Brule. It is true, the larger fish come out at night and forage for food. They will grab anything that moves on top of the water. The darker the night, the better the fishing. The fishermen use heavier bass-type rods and strong leaders for this. One good bait is a Hair Mouse. There is also one that looks like a frog. Large bass bugs are also especially good. You don't need a long line. You do need a guide that knows the river. It is easy to cast into bushes. On one occasion, I could hear a strange noise every time the fisherman would cast. I turned on the light, and behold the fly was hooked in the tie ring on the front of the canoe.

Rods and Reels

It is not my intention to give a technical discourse on trout fishing equipment. This is a big thing with many fishermen who enjoy top line tackle. Expensive rods are commonplace as are high-priced reels and lines. Expensive equipment does not "make the fisherman;" it is how he uses it. The same is true with the choice of trout flies. How it is fished ("wet" fly or "dry" fly) is most important.

Early in my career, I met an outstanding fisherman and fly tier supreme. Earl Grummett and his wife were experts at fly tying. They could duplicate any pattern you wanted. The flies were so well tied, you could fish without having them come apart like commercially-tied flies. Earl had one of his own that was an excellent pattern wet or dry. Earl offered to teach me his skill but I refused. I knew it took years to perfect this art. I have a fly vice and some materials but never got beyond the tying stage. I did get Earl to help start a club for some high school students.

Many men are fly tiers and enjoy catching trout on their own creations. One of my memories was a trip with Dr. Dave and wife Betty: great sports people with a love of the stream. On this occasion, Betty was doing needlepoint as Dave fished. By my standards, it was a good trout day but Dave was not having any luck. Betty said, "Dave, what kind of fly do you have on?" Dave replied, "I've got on a killer." (I had a hard time suppressing my laughter.) "Don't you think you should ask Larry (me) about the right choice?" replied Betty.

Every trout stream has its own special fly choices. It is, of course, related to the natural food typical of the stream. As I fish other area streams, this is so true (although some of the standard patterns will work on any stream if conditions are right). I fished some western streams and found they have special flies. A great sport for a fisherman is as they say "to match the hatch."

Several wet flies and dry flies are good producers on the Brule. Again, time of the year and the day will dictate what to use. Some of these patterns are very carefully guarded by some fishermen. We have only one fly my good fishing friend calls "old meat getter." If we need some fish for lunch, it will usually do the job.

One friend, George Koller, hand built some nice rods. He made some for some of my fishing friends. On one trip as we prepared to leave a landing, a Koller rod belonging to Dr. Vern Smith got hooked on something and snapped. I never forgot the Doctor's statement, "Anything I can replace with money, I don't worry about." I read a quote once that I liked very much, "More fish rods are broken in screen doors than on big fish."

One of my best fly rods was presented to me by a Catholic priest, Father Barta, who was associated with Boys' Town.

Brule Canoes: LaRock and Lucius

For a Brule fisherman, a canoe was a must (especially for the upper river). As I mentioned earlier, the Brule favorites were canoes built by Joe Lucius and John LaRock. They were of beautiful craftsmanship made of natural white cedar, with oak ribs and trim. They were mostly 18- to 20-footers. They had built-in live boxes and special low chairs. It was a comfortable canoe with a wide beam, very stable, nice to handle—they took rocks and handled very well. I could accommodate two fishermen who would change places now and then to afford the best fishing to the man in the bow.

From a not-so-practical side, they were heavy and harder to transport. Most of their use was strictly on the river.

I remember an old-time picture of these Brule canoes being handled by a horse-drawn vehicle like a hay rack. Some of these beauties are still in existence. The owners have kept them in good shape. Another disadvantage of a wooden canoe is the upkeep. Many of the old-time guides had winter employment refurbishing the canoes.

The whole picture changed with the advent of aluminum canoes. Fishing pressure increased and changed the number of fishermen and canoeists. Anyone could have a canoe that was tough and easy to transport. Some canvas-covered canoes ("Old Town") were used but not a good canoe for the average person fishing the Brule.

We were seeing more canoes on the stream, not all fishing but some for just pleasure. Selfish fishermen, we no longer had the stream to ourselves. Some old-timers took this pretty hard. It was years before they would purchase a metal canoe. It was fun to float by these lodges and see their fleet of canoes, all very nicely painted (usually green). One lodge had red; some were named mostly Indian names. Some lodges had eight or ten of these beautiful craft. They were kept in the water. Boat houses were built for winter storage.

These special canoes are now collector's items, even though most of them are still in use. Just a few years ago, I received my greatest gift from fishing friends. Dave Conolley and Ed Enichen, lodge owners, presented me with one of these special canoes. It has a special storage place and a special spot in my heart. I show it to my special friends. As a parting shot, Dave said, "For heaven sake, don't make a flower bed out of it when it gets old."

Some years before, I bought an 18-foot Gruman "guide model" canoe. It was portable and easy to handle, and I could carry it by car anywhere I wanted to go. I personally like wood but this was more practical. After over 40-some years, my Gruman is still in good shape. I didn't loan it out.

One of my friends, a novice canoeist, was angry because I didn't let him borrow it. I couldn't stand having someone bang it up.

When I first came to Brule, John LaRock offered to make me a canoe for $100—live box and all. I didn't have the money to splurge. It would be worth something today.

During one interesting summer, I had an unusual number of people for just canoe trips. I did the Stone's Bridge to Winneboujou route 12 days in a row. This is 15 miles by river. I get weary when I think of the canoe miles I have traveled up and down the Brule.

Some of my canoeing was poling. This is the way to ascend rapids. I learned that art from John LaRock, a master canoe man. The pole is about 10-feet long and is iron shod on the tip. You stand up in the canoe and plant your feet so you are steady as you pole.

A few rapids on the upper Brule require special handling by the canoeist. On one occasion as we came down the "falls," I noted the end of a green Old Towne canoe sticking out of the bushes. It proved to be only half of a canoe. They had gotten sideways in the "falls"—faster water did the rest.

Another time as we fished below the "falls," we noticed various pieces of equipment—paddles, life jackets, and a lunch box floating toward us. We knew someone had an encounter in the "falls." The "falls" were not life threatening but could make for a nasty day's outing.

Spare Parts

Most of the men brought extra rods and reels along. Occasionally, we had a "one rod man." I always carried a small kit with pliers, wire, and some spare parts. Rod glue came in handy on several occasions when I was able to repair a broken rod. I also saved more than one day by putting on new temporary line guides and rod tips. Spare leader came in handy also and ever present in my kit was mosquito dope.

Some fishermen wanted me to furnish equipment. This is not an easy thing to do. I did this for a few special friends.

I always carried a supply of Brule flies for people who were new to the Brule. Even some who were veteran fly fishermen realized certain streams had special flies. I never argued with a fisherman who had a favorite fly he liked to use.

While fishing with some Rockford, Illinois, people, we got caught in a summer rain. One lady in my canoe was dressed lightly and, as soon as she got wet, she became very cold. We headed for our lunch stop and built a fire. Part of my equipment was extra shirts and socks. She took off her blouse, and I helped her into a nice warm shirt. She said, "Button it for me." I took a lot of good-natured kidding from the rest of the gang.

Lady in canoe wears my extra shirt

A bad windstorm swept down the valley in the late 1980s. It totally destroyed our favorite Hidden Campsite and toppled some beautiful old-growth trees (some fell into the river making for better trout habitat). It did change the scenery in the Hidden area but the new tree growth is coming along fine.

Two of my fellow guides were at Hidden when the storm hit. They said it was a frightening experience but no one was injured. What saved the day was an axe we had stashed at the campsite. They used it to cut some trees that blocked the way.

A Guide's Story

No one has ever borrowed a cup of sugar from me but now and then I was asked for flies, leaders, and other equipment, and once was asked for a pound of bacon.

During my guiding days at the Degerman Lodge, I found that guides became very possessive of canoes and equipment. They didn't want other guides using their "stuff," even if it belonged to the lodge. Some guides went so far as to put initials on paddles. It is true that my own paddle had a special feel and was an important part of what I was doing.

I guess all sportsmen have some favorite equipment. Mine was an ordinary jackknife. It wasn't fancy, and I got it as a gift from one of my fishing friends. It had good steel and was just the right size for cleaning fish and doing other camp chores. It finally just wore out. I haven't found a good one since.

I used to carry a hand axe but cut out this practice because some fishing partners just love to hack up the forest for firewood, and I worried about them having an accident as well. I bring a bundle of wood from home; this works out better and saves our campsites.

While fishing the narrow upper Brule with Bob North, we encountered a deluge-type rain. The canoe started taking on some water. We had to go ashore to dump it. This was not easy because of the narrow stream and brushy shoreline. I am always mindful of things we fishermen put up with in the pursuit of trout.

Chapter 7

NATURAL BEAUTY

Fishing was my chief hobby, but next was my interest in the unique natural beauty characteristics of the Brule valley. Nature has done a special work here in flora and fauna.

One can see the effects of the glaciers. The old shorelines of the old glacial river are still in evidence, especially at Winneboujou. A special forest developed consisting of huge white and red pine. The upper river bog has a forest of balsam and spruce, with some hardwoods and "soft" mixed in. The bog itself is special: It covers a large part of the upper Brule to Big Lake. It acts like a large sponge which filters the drainage water and releases it slowly. This keeps the water at a stable level and keeps the water temperature cool, even in the hot days of August. This is important in making the Brule a great trout stream. Along bog areas, there are many springs that feed the river, improving water quality and cooling the temperature. Some of the springs, like McDougal, pump thousands of gallons of water into the river.

Years ago, some big timber was cut by Heinz and Weyerhauser. A few old trees were left standing in the bog, adding this diversity of old- growth trees to the Brule valley. These trees were important, providing nesting trees for the bald eagle and osprey.

I spent a lot of time learning about the interesting bog plants. The floor covering was the standard moss-like sphagnum. I thought the species of orchids were special. Pink and yellow lady slippers are common, but of special interest was the small yellow one that grew in only one small part of one of the bogs. I experienced some problems with this flower; my lady guests wanted to take them home. Several small orchids bloomed in season. My thought is that this bog is the lifeblood of the river. If it is not preserved, the Brule would just be a canoe stream.

Thought must be given to the areas close to watershed. Too much cutting in this area close to the stream could affect water quality and the fisheries, not to mention the aesthetics of the stream.

World record White Pine

We have some groups giving attention to the over-cutting and clear cutting in the Brule valley—notably, friends of the Brule River and Forest and the Lake Minnesuing Association. They are asking the State Forestry Department to limit cutting: No clear cutting and leave old-growth trees. These groups have been instrumental in passing a new forestry law to limit commercial cutting and show more interest in bio-diversity—that is, saving more of the forest for recreation.

Farther down in the bog area is Cedar Island. It has a large stand of white and red pine. This area shows what can happen with a little protection from man. This is one of the great natural sites of old-growth trees. Men like Henry Clay Pierce were farsighted enough to protect this timber for future generations.

At Cedar Island, we find some of the largest tamarack trees in our area. I am told that years ago in the early 1900s, an insect destroyed many large trees. A forestry man employed by Mr. Pierce painted bands of some material that prevented this fly from eating the foliage. The protective bands are still visible.

We are thankful to the early trout fishing families for purchasing and protecting this great resource. They have played an important part in protecting the Brule.

Some special plants have developed in the colder waters of the upper Brule. One is elodea—sometimes called water buttercup. In some springs, watercress is abundant. Some of the lakes on the Brule have weeds typical of other lakes, like musky weed.

Another flower that beautifies the Brule is the forget-me-not. This flower grows on rocks and logs in great profusion. This bloom is beautiful but it also gives off a delicate perfume. No attempt is made to remove these fallen logs from the river—only if they block the stream for passage of canoes. Fishery biologists say that logs in the stream help maintain good trout water.

The Brule supports an interesting population of birds because there are some old-growth trees suitable for nesting sites for eagles and osprey. It is not uncommon to see the eagle perched close to the river. The osprey is usually in flight or on the nesting tree. It is not uncommon to see the osprey dive into the river and bring up a fish. On occasion, one can see the eagle steal the osprey's catch by diving on him in mid-air.

I met a fisherman from Owatonna, Minnesota, whose

name was Reuben Kaplan. He was a great outdoorsman, and he fell in love with the Brule. He had fished and hunted all over the world and has written about some of his experiences.

The subject of eagles came up on our fishing trip together. I said we had a nesting pair on the Brule. (You could not see the nest from the river.) He said, "Can you show me the eagle's nest?" I knew he was testing me. We pulled the canoe out of the stream and walked a short distance to the eagle tree. The big bird was nearby—Reuben was satisfied. I have been tested several times by experts about my knowledge of the local flora and fauna, and I am proud to say that I have also learned from these people.

On several occasions while fishing, we noted a lot of birds of prey. The eagle has picked up surface fish very close to our canoe. It was common to see the osprey in action. Several times, we were close enough to see the osprey submerge and come up with a fish—usually a sucker, but on occasion a trout.

One day while I was fishing with a doctor friend, we heard terrific wind noise from a diving bird. It was the eagle dive-bombing an osprey who held a fish in his claws. The eagle made him drop it and the fish fell just a few feet from our canoe. The eagle continued his dive for the fish but veered when he saw our canoe. I am sure that he came back later for his catch. We often saw eagles and ospreys in battle. We would often see feathers flying and fish dropping into the river.

A most interesting event occurred while guiding a Mr. Schafer. He usually fished without his hearing aid. He used sign language to stop and go. On this one occasion, he wore his aid. He turned to me and said, "Do those damn birds always make so much noise?"

While guiding a man in the Cedar Island area on a windy day, there were a lot of woods noises. In particular, a hollow tree gave a moaning noise. My guest said, "I hear a cow. Is there a farm nearby?" I said, "The closest farm is about 10 miles from here." He didn't buy my tree noise explanation. "Guess I know a cow when I hear one," he said.

On windy days in this untouched forest, you can hear trees falling. On one occasion, a large dead tamarack fell dangerously close to our canoe.

Chickadees and bluejays are common the year around. One great summer bird is the white-throated sparrow. His song lends a nice, woodsy sound to the Brule. Several species of woodpeckers are also present. A nice sight is the pileated woodpecker with its accompanying drumming sound echoing in the valley. The old dead trees provide an ideal habitat for the bird.

The cedar wax wings are abundant during the fly hatches on the river. They will fly right over the canoe to catch flies. One fly catcher does its little song from the top of a high spruce. The guides insist his song is "Hip, hip, free beer." The bird book says something else.

Some bird watchers

There is a tremendous warbler migration in May. A few nest here such as the cape may warbler, myrtle, and northern

A Guide's Story

yellow throat. The nice little kinglets also nest here. Most of the small birds are hard to see because of the leafy trees along the bank of the river.

Water birds, like the blue and green herons, are quite common. Many small spotted sandpipers flit along the rocks and log. Mergansers, mallards, and wood ducks nest along the river. They can be seen along and under overhanging bushes.

The "river animals" such as mink, otter, and muskrats are also present. Beaver inhabit the upper reaches of the river and some tributaries. They can build dams in these narrow areas.

Bear are common, but hard to see because of the thick tree growth along the banks. Most of them are seen swimming across the river or at our campsites.

Some strange stories are told by some of the old-timers. One of the older Indian guides told of a large chunk of native copper near the headwaters of one of the large series of spring ponds on the Brule. I never could get the guide to go with me, and I never found it. I do have a large piece of drift copper from a Brule gravel pit, however.

When the snow comes, the Brule presents a whole new world. The canoeists have gone, and it is suddenly quiet. Now the winter birds and animals can be seen. If your timing is right, you might see brook trout spawning. Some duck are present before the little lakes and ponds ice over. On our last trip of the season, we might land at Hidden lunch grounds and build a fire to cook our meal. It is our last farewell to the river. We'll be back for the opening of the spring season.

Chapter 8

NOTES ON ECOLOGY

My guiding was not just fishing. A number of my clients were interested in preserving the natural environment of the Brule. The "nature lovers" were a nice change from the fishermen who wanted to spend long hours pursuing trout.

During the years spent on the Brule, I made a point to be familiar with all natural things on the river. In the 1940s, I was fortunate in being able to work with such outstanding specialists as John Thompson, Jr. (plant specialist from the University of Wisconsin), Dr. John O'Donnell and Dr. Hassler (biologists and fish surveyors).

Today's fishery biologists are well trained but many do not have the depth of background in the Brule River experience. It takes years to learn the secrets of the Brule. They would benefit from the years of Brule lore, which my fellow fishermen and guides could offer.

During the 1940s, I was asked to spend some time with a survey crew headed by John O'Donnell and Warren Churchill of the Wisconsin DNR. This survey was to check on the declining Brule fisheries. The new shocker method was used for stream sampling: complete biology stomach samples, water analysis, fish populations, summer water temperatures, examination of spawning beds, and spawning activities of the various trout species. Many specialists took part, adding their expertise. In all, it was a thorough examination of the Brule. For me, it was a fascinating experience. This survey was made available to the public. I am not sure that all of the recommendations were implemented by our DNR.

The Federal government got interested in the Brule in the late 1930s and 1940s. They hired a world-renowned trout expert, Sid Gordon. He was chosen to head a Brule River improvement program using CCC workers from the Brule camp. Stream deflectors built from rock were put in place to speed up the current. Bank shelters were also made to improve fish habitat. Some of these improvements are still to be seen along the river. A lot of controversy still exists about the value of these improvements.

When you look at stream improvements from the viewpoint of the fisherman, it must produce more fish! Many factors must be considered, such as the season, fish size, bag limits, and even fishing methods. We tried for years to get a fly-fishing-only section on the Brule. It was not a popular idea. In recent years, a fly-fishing-only section was added— that along with size limits, bag limits, creel census, and fish tagging is producing excellent results.

Of crucial importance now is the protecting of the Brule watershed. My friends and I feel that there is too much timber cutting in the Brule valley. We must think of retaining old-growth trees. Natural fallen logs and trees are also good for the stream to improve water quality and habitat.

Of great importance is protecting the large bog in the upper river. This, along with good forestry practices, will help keep the many springs active.

The organization of citizens (Friends of the Brule River and Forest and the Lake Minnesuing Organization) promotes forestry practices that protect the Brule and its watershed.

There is no question that we are overcutting our forests. The giant paper mills in our area are using up timber resources at an alarming rate.

Of special concern is the aim that the DNR has taken at the beaver population. The claim is that by damming streams, they create a silting problem that raises water temperature. I don't buy this 100%. The dams are short-lived and the river flow cleans out the old pond site. Some mighty fine fishing is found in the beaver ponds.

It would be amiss not to mention that the Brule is a great stream due to the early foresight of Cedar Island, Winneboujou Club, and other private property owners' efforts to keep the Brule in a natural state. The bog and forested area were not cut, and stream banks were kept wooded. The river flowing through these properties has retained its natural look.

Some of the best fly fishing on the river is in this natural area. We still have good fly hatches that make for sporty fishing.

Many of my fishing friends have expressed interest in programs to protect the Brule. Some years ago, Brule was required to put in a sewer system to protect water quality in the Brule River. I fished with an expert in the sanitation field. I showed him this system and he said, "It's not much of a system." He was correct as we were told recently the system must be upgraded.

Of special note: The Lamprey Program sponsored by the Federal, State, and Canadian commissions has done a fine job of controlling the lamprey population.

The Brule had become one of the largest lamprey spawning streams. A special dam was built on the lower Brule to prevent the lamprey going up the river to spawn. A chemical was used in the upper river and tributaries to kill the immature lampreys. This helped to restore the lake trout population in the Great Lakes, which had greatly diminished due to the killing of the trout by the lamprey.

In recent years, there was interest in the eagle "problem." Because spraying pesticides harmed the fertility of the eggs, very few young eaglets were born. I had a good chance to watch eagle activity in several nesting areas on the Brule. We now have more eagles in the area than ever before. They are fun to observe along the river. They would perch close to the stream, and one could really get a good look at this magnificent bird. Some of my fishing friends had a close-up look at an eagle for the first time.

Many bird watchers come to the upper Brule because its natural habitat is home to special birds. One expert bird man was a Wisconsin resident, Sam Robins. He was fun to be with, and I learned a lot about birds from him. Sam did not have to see the bird; he knew it by its song.

On one particular trip, Sam was looking for a specific bird. As we neared Cedar Island, he raised his hand and said, "That's the bird—a Cape May Warbler." Sam's intent was to prove that this bird nested in our area. I had two more later sightings of the bird near Stone's Bridge.

There were no guiding fees for this great "birder" Sam Robins. I considered my association with him to be a bonus to my guiding. Sam has recently published <u>Wisconsin Birds</u>. My daughter, Rene'e, presented me with a copy of this fabulous book.

Another outstanding day of "birding" was with a Federal judge from St. Paul. He was a guest of Vern Smith, and Vern delegated him to my care. It was a beautiful spring day, and we were seeing a large migration along the river. It was the peak of the warbler migration. I took the judge into McDougal Springs, away from the main stream. We saw warblers on every tree and fallen log. The air was alive with them. It was the largest migration that I have seen to date.

The judge was having a field day. He counted five new warblers for his lifetime list. He said, "This is one of my greatest bird-watching days. I don't care if we catch a fish."

Now that my guiding days are over, I reminisce about wonderful days spent on the stream with great fishermen and nature lovers. Most of these friends have passed on, but they have all left their mark on the Brule.

It is my hope that the many friends of the Brule and I have made a contribution toward the future of this great stream.

APPENDIX
MEL'S MIXED BAG
By Mel Ellis

A Man of the Brule

Brule, Wis.— There are no green pastures beckoning to Lawrence Berube, 41, schoolteacher, naturalist, fishing guide, carpenter, hunter, father—and well, you name it. He thinks there is no place in the world like the limestone cliffs which bulwark the state against the wild waters of Lake Superior; nor the endless barrens to the south; nor the red clay banks which hold the lower Brule; nor the upper river where the virgin timber shades Cedar Island—

Canada? Alaska? Not for Berube! He'll take his modern log cabin with the knotty pine interior, the one he built himself. He'll take the kids of Iron River, where he is school principal. And then when the kids get on his nerves, he'll be off upstream with a fine fly rod to try for another seven-pound rainbow like the one he caught a few years ago.

Companions of the Reel

He'll get hold of Jim Swanson, 22, one of his former pupils, and handle the boat while the young man tries to break the record again for a rainbow trout taken in the middle west on a dry fly. He did it in 1951 when he took the Field and Stream award for an 8 pound 12 ounce fish. He almost did it again in 1952 when he came in second with an 8 pound 5 ounce fish.

Maybe he'll look up old John LaRoc, guide for the presidents who've fished the Brule. Maybe they'll talk a little about how old John taught young Berube so much of what he knows about the famous river.

Or if it is summer, he'll probably be guiding, and if he's in the stern with the paddle and you are in the bow, there will be fish in the frying pan that night.

A Guide's Story

Maybe of an evening he'll compare notes with other Brule river guides in the restaurant which his wife operates. Maybe Steve and Max Weyandt will drop in. Perhaps it will be Jim Killoren, Ed Dennis, Cal Miller, Harold and Jim Swanson, Roy Lyons, or any of the other river guides pausing for a cup of coffee and a doughnut.

Leave the Brule

Leave Brule? Never! Why, where would a man find such hunting and fishing?

The residents of Brule would miss the jovial teacher, too. He's part of the village. When Gilbert Jorgenson got his leg about sawed off in a power saw, he was the man they called. A tourniquet stopped the bleeding. Then there was a wild ride to Superior. In the hospital there was the quart of blood running from Berube's veins into old Jorgenson's. And when the man began to regain consciousness, Berube looked over and said, "Well, you old Scandinavian, how does it feel to have a Frenchman's blood in your veins?" And old Jorgenson could smile even though the leg was gone by then.

Leave Brule? Why he is tradition there already. Old Frank, his father, built the foun-dation for that tradition. A resort operator on the Pike chain of lakes right outside of Iron River all his life, Frank is retired now to a home on the shores of that same chain.

The Roots are Deep

Leave Brule? After putting his roots down so deep— deeper even than the big trees—down into lives of the people who call a river home?

Not Lawrence Berube! He'll take the winter winds and the pelting snow, and the rutted roads and the high water and the damp and gloom. Because after the dark days come the sunny days, and after the barren weeks the green months, and when the hardwoods color up in the fall and the air is crisp and the mist lifts like campfire smoke, there's a feeling wells up inside a man that wants to make him take off through the woods singing so there'll be no wild thing waiting around for his gun.

No Berube won't leave the Brule. Not until his judgment day, and then if he lives to be as old as John LaRoc he'll be as much a part of the river as the rocks it rolls over.

(Taken from the <u>Milwaukee Journal</u>, 1954)

June 19, 1972

In addition to these records, my mind was haunted by memories of several canoeing trips on the Brule River in eastern Douglas County between 1961 and 1965 when I had heard birds that did not sound quite right for Black-and-White Warblers and so had gone unrecorded. Could any of these have been Cape Mays? Riding in one of John Degerman's canoes, piloted expertly by Lawrence Burbe, my wife Shirley and I made the trip from Stone's Bridge to Winneboujou on June 28, 1973, and found singing Cape Mays at three locations.

A note from the Wisconsin Bird Book "The Passing Pigeon" by Sam Robbins, June 11, 1969.

Brule Notes

Some years ago, we built a retirement home — where else, but on the Little Brule and Sandy Run fork ... I can boast that two trout streams cross my property. The Brule itself is just a few blocks away.

One of my fishing friends was an architect — Hilman Estenson. He helped us design a house that fit the Brule area, including a living room with large glass doors across one wall which looks out over the small trout valley. It's woodsy, and we have all the animals and birds that go with each change of seasons.

My oldest guide friend was Antoine Dennis, a Chippewa and a fine, interesting gentleman. He told me that the spot where I built my house was a famous camping place for Indians. I have looked for signs but have found none. My closest neighbor found an arrowhead. It is pleasant knowing that they camped here and fished "my" stream.

We have an interesting arrangement with Ed Enichen, a long time Brule fly fisherman from Rockford, Illinois. Ed has a love for rhubarb pie. It so happened we have a rhubarb patch and my wife Millie is an expert pie baker. Ed sees that we have a nice meal of brookies and gets a pie. Ed releases most of his fish.

One day on a guiding trip we encountered the U.S. Fish and Wildlife team treating the Brule for lamprey control. A brilliant green dye was put in the stream to check the volume flow — this enabled them to put in the correct amount of chemicals to kill the small lamprey. The river reminded me of a famous soda that I liked when I was young, Green River. The most interesting thing about the Green River — it did not affect our fishing. We had a normal, good fishing day.

While fishing with George one day in the Cedar Island area, we camp upon a nice man and his wife exploring the stream. George made a few remarks about the fact that they were spoiling his fishing. He could not believe you could enjoy the Brule without being a fisherman. The nice man politely replied, "I guess you don't own the stream." I was very embarrassed and managed to give the couple a happy sign to show how I felt.

I fished with a man who was a syndicated writer. He was also employed by several large companies. He was an eastern trout fisherman anxious to see what the Brule was like. He quizzed me the entire day about my life style for his newspaper column. It was very interesting, we had a good fishing day.

Recently a man came to Brule to see the summer homes along the Brule. He said he saved his picture and materials until he needed an article.

A young man who left the Brule some years ago and became a very successful businessman said, "Paddle me down from Stones to Highway B as fast as you can." A strange request but I obeyed.

I had several fishing friends who like to fish the White River. We would do it by canoe and during the evening fly hatches. The brown fishing was usually good.

I had a bad experience with a car. Bob North wanted me to start at the chimney on the upper river — a low, rutty road. He ruined my whole muffler system — over one hundred dollars.

While fishing with my nice Dr. Gracey and his wife, we stopped at a small dock jutting out into the Brule. To get a better picture, Dr. backed off the dock but managed to hold his camera out of the water.

We stopped at our favorite hidden lunch grounds and found a nice fishermans vest hanging on the screen house. As we were out eating our lunch we saw a canoe enter our inlet in great haste. A man got out of the canoe, took the vest and left without a word.

It amazed us to find neat little bags of garbage at our lunch place. We had signs, "If you brought it with you, take it home."

My fishing friend Bob set himself up as a doctor — he has a special bag with medical supplies.

One day while fishing the Upper Brule at the Stone Chimney, we heard an unusual motor sound. I said, "It sounds like an outboard motor." They are banned on the River. The occupant turned out to be some special biologist. We had a lively conversation about using motors on the Brule.

My guiding companion Jim Swanson was with some

guests from New York. They were not fishing people and the conversation was different. The conversation was especially interesting — "I say, have you been to the opera lately?"

A good fishing friend was Dr. Thorson, who taught dental surgery at the University of Minnesota. Dr. came with a new movie camera. He said, "I hope I can get some great shots." As we rounded a corner, an eagle was sitting on a big log eating a large trout. This Dr.'s camera is in a nice leather case. I would class it as a once in a lifetime picture.

A morning ritual with Dr. Vern Smith's party was a toast to the Gods of Nature with orange juice. It was a Norwegian "Solar Upper". After the first toast I learned that the orange juice was "fortified".

The use of innertubes to float the Brule became a serious problem. The "tubers" could not control their craft and would bump into canoes and wading fishermen. It took a lot of organizations and finally legislation to stop the tubing. The other big problem was leaving containers of garbage along the stream.

On one occasion we were exploring McDougal Springs. My guests were the Crosby sisters from a well known Brule family. The spring is about five feet below the water surface. It boils the water surface. It boils up from the bottom in a large splurge of white sand pouring a large amount of water into the Brule. After gazing at it for a few minutes one girl said, "I would like to take off my clothes and immerse myself in this beautiful spring." Of course it didn't happen.

I thought it would be interesting to find the origin of some of our good flies. Of particular interest was the Pass Lake. After some inquiries a lady wrote us and told us her grandfather named it many years ago. The history of using flies I guess goes back to the Egyptians.

My daughter recently found a book of most of the known flies in color — very interesting. My daughters would go into hysterics when I told them the fly that we caught our fish on today was Rat Face McDougle.

It was pleasure to watch Earl Grummett tie his beautiful fly patterns. Earl's special fly was called "arrowhead". It could be fished wet or dry and was excellent on the Brule. I am sure it was an original with Earl. By the way, Mrs. Grummett was a super fly tyer.

I would be amiss not to mention my acquaintance with the "Dean" of the old time Brule fishermen, Dr. Arthur Holbrook. His fishing spanned some of the "Golden Years" of trout fishing on the Brule. He maintained his beautiful trout lodge "Gitchee Gummee" for his family and friends. It is still in use by the family. When the Dr. retired, he would spend the entire summer fishing with his guide Ed Dennis. His log for one summer was ninety six days on the Brule. He kept a record of number of size of his fish. The limit was large and his catch for the summer was very impressive. He gave his data to the biologists to help study the Brule. He played a big part in helping to keep the Upper Brule in a wild natural state.

Another great friend of the Brule was Haskell Noyes. He served on the conservation commission for several years. He did much to promote good legislation to protect our trout streams and wildlife.

I asked Antoine Dennis how the native Americans fished the Brule. He stated, "They carried hooks and line and for a rod they cut a sapling. For a lure they used a small piece of red flannel - caught a trout everytime." They fished only for food - I never had the courage to try this method.

As I think back over my years of guiding, I had become a fly fishing guide, only I knew some great men who enjoyed spinners and bait. I became a reformer - changing these men to the art of fly fishing. Most of these fishermen found trout fishing more enjoyable - they could tie their own flies and buy expensive equipment.

One of my oldest friends didn't want it to be known that

he had been a bait fisherman - he had even used salmon eggs.

A special mention must be made about the Brule Sportsmen's Club. They are doing a great job of improving the Brule fishery. The Club is presently engaged in habitat improvement.

A Brule Story

I would like to make some comments on my favorite subject — the Brule River.

I speak as an "Old timer" having spent most of my lifetime living in the Brule area. I was an active Brule fishing guide for over fifty years. My fishing friends came from all over the United States and several foreign countries. They came to the Brule to fish and enjoy this great natural stream. One man once stated, "I didn't think there was a place left in the world like the Upper Brule River." Many outdoor writers have mentioned the natural beauty of the Brule.

In recent years, some of my friends of the Brule became alarmed about timber cutting in the Brule watershed. Some cutting was very close to the stream. Our days on the streams were marked by logging activities so close we could see the activity and hear the noisy machinery.

We also noted some of the plots were clear cut. Spray was even used to kill off a stand of oak trees close to the River. These practices were questioned by my friends and we talked to the DNR, but our concerns were not answered.

In several early Brule River surveys, mention was made not to cut too close to the River, and in fact, to protect the whole watershed.

Biologists have stressed the idea of leaving "old growth trees" in the Valley. They also mentioned the value of leaving logs and woods in the River to help unsure water quality and habitat for fish and animals. If it were not for the fine forestry management of Cedar Island and Winneboujou properties, there would not be good trees for nesting eagles and osprey in the Brule Valley.

I think some thought should be given to some scattered type of planting; not all pine plantations. For instance, hardwoods and food-bearing shrubs would be beneficial for the birds and animals. It would also be good to let some of the aspen plots mature and die in hope some native trees: spruce, balsam and white pine would flourish. Many other plants and flowers would grow in such a forest. It would make for a natural forest.

Our citizen groups, The Minnesuing Association and Friends of the Brule River and Forest, have come forward with the new concept of a forest for everyone. With the help of State Representatives, Frank Boyle and Dr. Wayne Johnsrud, and attorney, Walter Kuhlmann, a new forestry bill was passed that is in line with our thinking on better forestry management.

It is pleasing to note that it was easily passed through the legislature process and was signed by our Governor.

It is the hope of my friends that we can work with the Forestry people in implementing this law. We plan to play a part in formulating a new master plan for our State Forest.

As a final thought, It is "our Forest and our River", and it is about time we came forward to help preserve this great valley of the Brule.

An article written for "Splinters" a friends of the Brule Publication.

Laurence Berube

Song Of The Brule

Words and Music by WILLIAM S. SYLVESTER
Harmony by L. Caldwell

1. You have heard the song of riv - ers, and of stream,
2. Here the Birch-es, Spruce and Pine so state - ly rise,
3. Here the wild-life of the for - est safe - ly hide,

Made im - mor - tal by some po - et sing - er's theme,
Like Ca-thed-rals, or as tem-ples made by God,
Here the wild birds in the tree-tops burst in song,

But when writ-ten down to date, There's a stream that now is great,
Where to wor-ship is to pray: There to seek our God each day,
Here the heart with strength grows strong For the batt-les o - ver wrong,

Since "Cal" Cool-idge came to fish up - on the Brule.
Where the moss is green on banks be - side the Brule.
While the rap - ids dash their spray a - long the Brule.

Refrain:

Oh, the song of the Brule I am sing - ing, Ca-

A Guide's Story

SOME BRULE FLIES

Arrowhead

Royal Coachman

Gold Ribbed Hare's Ear

Irresistible

Pass Lake

Royal Coachman

Rat Face McDougal

A Guide's Story

7-10-84 — Great catch of trout

Large brown trout

All set for a day on the Brule

All set for a Brule trip

A Guide's Story

A nice catch ready for the frying pan

Lawrence and Bob with a nice Brown Trout

A night visitor on the Brule

Rustic bridge at Cedar Island

A Guide's Story